Peace Petals

MANDOVI

Copyright © 2023 by Madhumita Mahato

All rights reserved.

This book or any portion thereof may not be reproduced or used in any manner whatsoever without the express written permission of the respective writer of the respective content except for the use of brief quotations in a book review.

The writer of the respective work holds sole responsibility for the originality of the content and The Write Order is not responsible in any way whatsoever.

Printed in India

ISBN: 978-93-6045-870-6
First Printing, 2023

The Write Order
A division of Nasadiya Technologies Private Ltd.
Koramangala, Bengaluru
Karnataka-560029

THE WRITE ORDER PUBLICATIONS.

www.thewriteorder.com

Edited by Ridham Bassi

Typeset by MAP Systems, Bengaluru

Book Cover designed by Nikhil Kamath

Publishing Consultant - Samyuktha Prasanan

Dedication

This book is dedicated in memory of my beloved mother, the Late Mrs. Chandra Devi, who was a great motivator for my literary endeavours.

FOR PEACE - FLOWERS

Without and within,
The power of harmony, peace; reign.

That is, was, and has been
The most sought after essence,
Since dawn of eternity
To begin,

To build it upon
In everything,
Let that really mean.

Every way we act in,
Deal, behave, and spread it,

For coolness of peace,
Should all be keen.

Believe, imbibe,
Love, and live it.

So, promise it,
Those at helms—
Let it, the rulers' and of the ruled
very breath be.

Be it the guide,
We do upon it lean.

To make it the most
Potent reason, means,
Calms and contentment serene.

Only then can nations
All flourish, shine,
And all good things happen,
Or else, we pine.

So, hands I fold,
May it happen for peace,
To bloom flowers, embellish,
Not only on bridal veiled buns,
But on bayonets, blossom!

Madhumita Mahato 'Mandovi'

WHERE FIND SHINE

The going is tough,
It ought to be,
But it's undoubtedly too rough.

We are the berserk.
The real 'We' on roads,
For whom, it's all sweat—
Head to toe.

Why for thrusted
Into a fiery blow?
Why forced to cast
As a voter at the polls?
Midst fear of life, the
Trivial, showdown-row.

Sacred dip all, at once
Is as costlier though.

Why life mingling,
Merged in crowds, of
Wedding buffet rows?
Who to answer such woes?

Destiny falls behind
Man-made structured doom
of nature—

Earth, water, the green;
The sky, air, the sound,
Its rains in line,
Leaving us harrowed!

Oh! Thoughtless devastation of earth!
Where should we run,
Get safe, hide?

How good will turn
depleting loss
of man's bubble—pride?

But where shall find that
Inspirational shine?

Dwindling, ravaged
We pine.

Awaiting, arise of that
Assured Divinity
In humans, sublime!

EVERGREEN

Evergreen,
Those haunts
of flowery hills/meadows, rivulets.
Lose no charm in snow,
or at times basked in a sunny glow.

Evergreen,
The koel's numbers,
Waking up in dawns
of lazy slumber.

Evergreen,
Her sleepy hums,
My mama's calmly charms,
Making me smile even in glum.

Evergreen,
The bro's successes
Whose ambitious horizons
Fail their access.

Evergreen,
The dictionary,
My books,
Being teachers, these matter.

But a student still in middle age,
Evergreen I, new to life,
Still a starter.

Evergreen,
This life, its cycle.
That is and remains
As the only pristine, evergreen, eternal miracle.

WHAT'S AMISS, THAT WAS

Distant years ago
We, in nature, lived conformed.

Humans breathed not in mad race,
But well-timed with nature,
Strode in balance.

Nature graced earth,
Peace in reign.

Rose and shone
The balmy sun,
The cool blue, the lively green.

Nature at its best;
Our mother, fresh with concern,
Us blessed.

Humans paused and were not
In this, now infamous,
Neck-break run.

Nature, though raged at times,
Still nurtured, casting
Teacher's care, only for
Her kids' welfare.
Patience in abundance

And at times impatience,
Helped build cities,
Dynasties, greatness;
Only in natural consonance.

Great thoughtfulness,
Grave sincerity,
Gritty conformed practices,
Helped build, vibrant
Humanity's edifice.

Prevailing harmony,
Confirming peace.

They moved yet,
In life, challenged
With gaily ease.

Green was the scene.
He pleased, found meaning
In all, and with all beings.

I ponder how now,
We fall short of
Any such obedience.

Gasping, sizzling, sorrowful,
Lost in futile wants, we.

Where there is 'everything',
But with the 'soul' missing!

BOOKS - ALL LOOKS

Books are a look
Into the mysteries of life;

Are of rainbow hues,
Leaving impressions,
Its memorable clues;

Windows to the world
They depict, describe
Decipher, display,
Various variants of variable life
That may shock, surprise;

Ardently summarize—
stories/novels/plays/poems,
portraying variations in life,
novel vagaries on display.

Stories popular, pull public;
That ring, in romantic may,
Or sob in tragic dismay—
It offers various arrays.

The science-fiction, best seller,
Plunging into space.
May be, the 'tough Holmes'
Solving an intriguing case.

The magical broom, the sorcerer,
Children should not miss.

Or the psycho thriller, spreading the 'hiss'.

The arena of Philosophy,
Life-lessons,
Choice is yours.

You can also score as
Armchair traveller of
The distant Mediterranean shores.

History books, stories of
Personalities/societies,
Peaking possibilities;
Which any enthusiast
Just might imbibe.

Also must and just
The text books, for
Intelligent reading.

Also gaining from prized
Encyclopaedia,
All sized dictionaries.

Map books, or school's
Own logbooks,
Maybe just flipped over.
The rest are for diligent study, I'm sure!

Cook-books are delicacies,
And so are gardening,
Embroidery—all such
And more; passions, hobbies.

Fashion books on hands of
Fashionista, glee,
Fashion designing, or
Interior decoration, may be.

More still, exam guide books, shine bright,
For success, to overcome any fright.

So, to know, feel and live
Full well the good life of delight.

Wishing you all,
Good words, good books,
And an exciting world
Of literary affinity, respite.

SORROWS AND LESSONS

Sorrows not only try
Impatiently to morose,
But wish to be
Made known to all.

Or, silently, secretly,
Unhappily seclude.
As some try to hide
Behind a veil of patient tears.

Through its literary expressions,
It may become a matter of,
Exciting, interesting, absorbing,
Wonderful explorations.

Glumness will however
Not usher much harm really,
As it's an effect not cause,
You may see!

But, surely its deadly,
By making one with it
Unarmed, though seemingly.

So shrug it off,
Than giving inclusion.
And present normal life
In every situation.

Better leave
Glumness in seclusion.
But try poise,
Make no gloomy fusion.

It may, mock matter be,
If revealed
Everywhere, among all,
Unless those, humane, reasonable.

Though there is still
A listening heart in crowds,
That believes in you,
Stands apart.

It calls for, as must,
Any mitigation.

Let it not be the master,
Better let it
The slave be.

However,
Tutoring tolerance at start,
Also, must lesson
of patience they impart.

They grant lessons
of laughing away troubles,
so as to fail to double.

Educates, oblivion of ill-wills,
While teaching forgiveness.
So as, are same to receive.

Not behave haughtily, proud,
Or brag success loud,
But to live humbled.

For who knows,
What, who, which,
Will soon us leave.

Thrashing us, breaking us,
Leaving us flat on our face! Stumbled!
Thereafter, yes, only humbled!

Loving all willingly,
Living cheerful, loved;
Will only impart,
A pool of well-wishers, smart.
To tide over troubles if they start.

So, come on,
Look in the face of it,
You 'big heart'!

Counter, fight, defeat
Deadly sorrows,
As you might, and repeat.

For a life of hope,
Cheerful resilience-glow.

Be victor
Already today,
Or still even,
Live gaily tomorrow!

WAY TO LIVE

Faring well in a fair life,
Is as important
As its farewell.

Its worth nor its nature,
It belies,
With teeming crowds
And the rolling teary eyes.

Your star-lit palms,
Held out to innocence,
The ailing;
And not only
Rocketing successes,
Do count.

Happiness - a ball shared,
Spread many times around;
Endear quick returns;
That may leave us spellbound.

So do pains, injected, inflicted,
Always severely rebound.

Spreading pleasures, pleasurable,
Add immunity counts.
As friendship, gestures, jokes,
Simply, let go.

All lively jigs,
Livening the bored spirit.
Happy colorful strokes
of paints,
maybe, naughty, loving expressions, displays.

A soul becomes great
Only with gratefulness,
That accepts accolades well.

If only re – offers bestowing,
As sky – gifts, heaven – owings.

All sincere efforts.
Will follow such.
Will never be shied.
Also its fruits
Always delight,
But only delay, they might.

A heartfelt obedience,
Obeisance to Divinity,
Is the essence.

Your life-account
Is only just accurate,
As at heaven's gate.

Improvised, only by
Its 'karma', and imposed.
But surely can be improved,
With all that's done "Good".

That's it!
Sounds, sense
You get
Is open to all debate!

You cannot block it,
Though delay.
With must essential, Mom nature's
Cause-effect formula,
As sole player, to stay.

So let goodness,
Your guidance be.

Spread cheer,
Even with a heart heavy.
And let life be,
Your own, contentment story.

TELL A TALE

'Once upon a time…'
Is not only a phrase,
It's an extension
of the writer's self, personality,
of his world, of his cosmos,
In parts, in totality.

And all that he knew, knows,
To express and so
Faith on his pen, he does repose.

It'll open you to old reactions,
New responses.
How the social world
You would like to explore.

What shocks 'in hands' at first,
Many stereotypes, myths,
Archaic, pedantic habits burst.

Is only normal, new or neo normal yet,
Actually, the way you see it.
In a fluxing society, this.
of which it also, a mirror is!

Desperation in 'How Much Land Does a Man Require?'
Spun by Leo Tolstoy;
Makes you weary.
Man's predicament,
His hope, unfailing,
At times, leaves him
Dead gasping.

The 'Gift of The Magi' of O Henry
Tells tale of gifting,
Its ardour:
Results in disbelief, dismay,
Remains a tale of
Ingenuous adoration
of an awestruck score.

Maupassant's 'The Necklace'
Turns pleasant the jeopardy,
Easing, burden of its misplace.

Thought of the era,
The aura, of the story,
The plot, character, place,
Exceeds the sequence
Maybe even time, space.

Girl's fancies and 'Twenty-Six Men and a Girl'
Penned by Gorky.
The swagger, of the swain
Their swank.
Or eerie 'The Pot of Basil'

of Giovanni,
Leaves us in, a gape, blank.

All swamp the mind's crevices,
Stories, and their ongoing
Debate on virtues and vices.

Every tale is telltale.
Do you want to listen to more?

The spin a tale, spin wheel
Is here to spin tales, galore.

Would you like to stop by
At this story's lane?
Are you sure?

MOM MINE

You've embarked me
Upon the journey of life.
You've brought me on,
Up there with loving firmness.

Your nectar—my gift of life,
Never in excess, always rife.

Your charmed imprints on me,
Passionate signs, your design.
Glint of those eyes,
On my first smile;
Yet shows in your wrinkles.
Smile, that still glows
Warmly on cheeks of mine.

Your cajoles cold rebukes well conceived,
Surpass in elan else all;
What exactly the soul seeks.

You're ever there,
Full, in favour.
You, my heartful solace,
Together we've been
In most tough places;
Held closely by you
With great love caresses.

Mother, dearest dear,
Why do you reign!
How well you respond!
Are able to feel, so intense;
You, my queen!
What draws us so near,
I know not.
But always love you lots.

This instinct, well-known bond,
Holding more than whatever strong,

Your boon, and your blessings
Where all worries dump in soft ease,

Your warm arms clasping tight,
From here, care finds no escape:
Your concern, undefeated, infinite.
Mom! My land enchanted,
My 'garden of faith';
My loving, sprinkling
Spring in splashes;
My harvest of happiness.
I count on you,
More than God, no else!

WHEN WIN DOESN'T MEAN

Wins are often likened to
Intoxication,
Causing brutal wars,
Unjust upheavals,
Maybe, righteous uprisings.

May prompt elaborate
Plans, design when truth evasive,
Intrigues, connivances unsuitable.

Or maybe of wars hoary, recent,
Lead by kings/generals,
Gallery of nobles.

As of now,
Lure of victory
Fueling greed,
Promoting freebies
For election seat—'House' tables.

People struggle, fight
Jostle with each other, push,
Pull things, throw.
The battle/struggle scene;
To be victor,
Isn't always pleasant show.
Yet not always so.

Win isn't all; for the 'noble' all,
That we know.

Victor Ashoka's might for peace
Here, confirms the state.
Win, for the great astute,
Rose from grief/victorious Ashoka.

Spinning him to Dhamma,
Heralding prosperity, peace.
Pulling curtains on bloody drama.

Need of this hour
Pausing war, annulling peace,
Wars awaiting full stop, comma.
Yet seeking less compromise,
With elastic 'thank you', 'please'.

Great Alexander needs mention must,
Winning, by Chenab banks
Losing to bravery yet, its ranks!

All victorious,
But unlike his nature,
Uttering 'thanks' to foe.
For the lesson,
Enriching gallant yearn.

No one won
In this battle of equals.
White sun of tranquillity shone.

If victory heralds downfall,
Equals defeat.
If blazes the trail of life lessons, hopes,
Is your win, if it doesn't involve sin.

If are not so, the hopes one pins;
Beware as Kauravas
In lack of goodness
Forsaken by history,
Died languid, leaving no kin.
No one to cry on,
Wipe tears there in.

Take heart, be with the
Just sum of means and ends.
This value in all ages truly trends!

So, righteous you be in all,
Even small battles, victory.
That's simply 'great'
You see!

SHE, STATE, STRENGTHS

What's there in depths
Of shy feminine demeanour,
She's often not candid about,
Though herself sure.

She veils,
Sensitively, ideals;
Desires, problems, loss, grief,
Love, the forsakes,
More often than not.

Sometimes of will,
Mostly for traditions resorted to.
The veiled life, look,
Prompted in past;
By enemy attacks,
The ravage, ransom, rape, kill.

The veil, held tightly then,
Has turned flimsy,
Has slipped away
For good or evil,
As it, you see.

Of times now, it's
Marred, destroyed along
With the colony of

feminine yearns, wishes.
Hopes, plans gone disarray;
Shattered now, not by the 'hack',
But appalling acid attacks,
Scarring body, mind, spirit.

But gentle, the resolved heart,
Betters by accounting wrong,
Counting hopes.
Where love, care still holds.
Ever only rarely does show.

The inequality index,
Foeticide, infanticide,
Underage marriages, dowry deaths,
Flouting female dignity;
Killings associated.

Fair treatment, puts off;
When comes to even government 'houses'
As very unjustly this falls.
Now seems to scale up, stays.

As if girls and women are rubber dolls.
Will always bear all with a smile;
However skewed.
As if are there only to rue,
Never creating any rustle, cry, or hue.

Take heart girls, now
You're opening wings
Onto skies, both blazing/blue.

Inducted in the airforce, navy, army;
Can bomb out any enemy.
Fight, swim, fly;
Can flex our sinews of body, mind,
Not making any shy.

To take note it's must
Women are best, in whatever they do.
Be it any position, avenue—
The mother, boss, doctor,
The minister, to name a few.
Found less, but the best
In the list of who's who.

Women wisely never enter
Unsure, useless, blame game.
We know moreover, every
Thoughtlessness is the same.
This unfairness, we heavily slam.

To feel slight at every step,
Really is disheartening,
To feel, live—
Learn from us,
Still never give up!

With resolved calms,
Walk, forge, fight, fly,
Whichever to fairness deny.
With your unarming scorns, smiles,
You, my blessed
Ladies, of emboldened might!

Keep in mind, the others!
Think awhile,
We, are power towers,
Don't you think dolls-fragile.

MY SON, MY LOVE

My son, my fascinating adore,
My fun, fame and fiesta galore!

Your radiant smile
Enters my heart's doors
And its effulgent waves
Find in you,
Their innocent shores!

Any work, school, home,
Any chore,
For you, I am not
So busy.
To attend always,
My heart assures.

Your every call stands tall.
The moment I attend,
Now, it calls for even more.
But, not trifle impatient me,
Holding you tight,
Loving, sure!

This wish, since days of yore,
Now in me, has
Found its soil-secure.
My fruitfulness, meaningful,
For 'You' the fruit it bore.

Some blessings, I always save,
Mom's wishes heartiest, hopes untiring.
Blessed, careful dreams scored.
My thumping heart,
For you, its great love,
Ever showers, surrounds, stores!

WHY FEAR

If you aim for the sky
Why fear, why 'why'?
The dawning sun
Can't be stopped.
Night turns to day.
What, when can happen,
Who ever can say?
What you can do;
Who knows but you!
Turn every stone
And you will be known
For who you are!
Just give your 'will' a chance,
Fight open veils of doubt
Don't be shy!
So, you do dare try!
Why fear, why shy?

EACH DAY'S HOPE

When pain strikes,
Who but 'You'
Whom my heart seeks.
My soul afloat in sail
Knows who else,
But your shores,
To tide all anxieties.
I ardently long
Your gracious doors.
Your tenderest care,
My heart seeks always.
Where puny unhappiness,
In titbits of my mundane life,
Find in despair, solace!
Just be there, stay,
My weary heart, pins
Each day's hope.
To You, I pray!

IQBAL, THE VALOROUS

Glorious village
Where he was born,
The very home
Where his youth was blown;
Drew slowly out
A desire in him, unbent,
To break open 'silent towers'
of vacant sounds
And dumb wishes.

To bloom, blaze out
All run-ups,
Striking all types of pitches.
Struck out of mundanity,
Made it this day.

He is ready,
Unspoken of word,
Unheard of fame,
Strong and strident,
Blazing his run-up
Like a gazelle
In gaining gallop.

His bold release,
His handed sphere,
Talking to breeze

Kissing crease,
Jolting the other
To the sole defensive gear.

This 'the' match for
The silent, mute boy.
Heart burning with zest,
Putting all his skills to test,
Foretelling his next big fall;
Blasting ball after ball.

His worked up attack
Gaspingly praised,
Witnessing ruins of defense
Burnt to ashes.

His strong grasp,
The glinting cup awaiting handle,
Eyes jolly, tearful,
Raising his gold cupped hands
In a soulful mumble.
As crowds went thunder,
All roaring, as palms
Waving to that valorous boy,
Budged and bowed
In quiet surrender!

BINOD – TO LIVE DREAMS FOR OTHERS

Beneath date trees,
Under the sun sparkling,
In waters blue of pond pristine,
As splashed in may
Little Binod—in frolic display.

Growing up, nothing much
Got them to spare
From his toils intense,
At a little farm, his father's.

His mother, with care all,
Stacked sum a little,
From their puny income
For little Binod's school–run.

Astride in 'boldness' he,
Covered miles daily,
Didn't count how many;
To school-secondary, far in town.
Yet fortune was only in frown.

But zestful, little 'big heart',
Sought no excuse nor plea,
Nor wanting a coward's flee.
Dauntless, bright, went in flight,
Gazing stars, starlit-eyed.

Went off so, after school,
For two ends a meet.
Joined as a clerk at the office,
Where insults were in bits
But little fees.

Took it as challenge to be,
When insult hurled at him,
For self-respect to keep,
And answer potent, to befit.
The cursed job left he.
No one much noticed,
But later, all to see.

Moved on in life,
Studious, his intent,
With patient diligence.
Passed college, and on he went.
Strode he promising,
To make career of the day—
A lawyer's degree.

Knew he well, money's deciding,
And made much of it, as
In collieries investing.
Set out he, on task uphill
To live not for self, only.
Bring change, to lives, be.

For care, concern real,
Welfare social, as also uplift,
A life, tireless, dedicated to be.

For the needy, charged zero fee.
Also lakhs he pardoned
On request earnestly, so many.
A thing no modern day lawyer
Will wish to do even in dreams.
So, today this can't be.

Score or so, learning centres
Founded, an 'institution' he.
A university stands in his name today,
As homage to him we pay.

Cared he from heart,
People to serve, only.
No lip-service, so
Didn't make Binod weary.

Practising mighty charity,
Fees entire for education,
Marriage of daughters dear,
Diseases, demises, or even
If the farmer's ox dies.

Was always there,
Holding no bias,
Held out his heart.
That's fair.

His aspiration, lofty,
To forge, surge, fight out.
Away mistreatment!

To carve out the 'promised land'
For his people-excruciating.

Where light, hope,
Fairness, concord reign.
Liberty meets equality, its twain.

Heroic sheet anchor
Of the 'promised land';
People didn't forget,
even after untimely,
Plaintive, his death.

When thousands stood sobbing
For their hero, benevolent,
As in love, dirge reciprocated.

Finally, the 'promised land'
Was carved to be.
Yet, sadly awaits lots,
For his noble dreams to realize,
People's glee.

Do you too adhere to
A vision,
Want to try?
That you can also,
If you strive,
And you can,
Your any, any
Dreams live by!

LOVE PURE

What's in this flimsy frame,
But a soul palpable, loving?
—A great masterpiece
of mastery Divine.
Yet it's mortal.
But surely can feel,
Register bliss!

Nothing to be vain about by
Thinking it 'be all' or 'end all' to be.
We're nothing, but
Divine lasting dreams forever.
In pure creation, 'His'.
That we are ordained to live.

The love showers
From 'His' bowers
Upon us, from up above;
Is a rare, grateful offer.

Your glint, glaze from eyes loving
For the beloved,
Is but a glimpse of that love Divine.
If its pure pristine
With the glinting
Unconditional shine.
Waiting of eternity,

Parting of souls sublime,
That again meet on the
Shores of eternal time.
Not accidentally, but
With a promise in design.
Destiny, it has to be.

Not known to us, as we are
But his loved 'instruments', you see.

Souls we, now in search,
Afloat on waves of time,
Flitting, flying.
Who, when, for how long
Shall meet us,
And knowing not why?

Sooner, to unravel treasure troves.
As the drunken bee, stops a while
For the ephemeral flower
Blooming in eternity.
However continues
Journey ongoing,
Taking flight
On moments' wings
As it spans the endless sky.

THE TWO ON RIDE

Machine on glide,
Child hunched on
Held it tight.

Joy overflowing
For his new-found ride.
Freedom freshly found,
Sparkling on his form.
Shaking sometimes,
Sometimes straight,
For it to end,
He will not wait.

Gleeful and gritty
As he rode,
Forgotten moments
In me, he arose.
My heart's thumping
And its joys;
How as a boy,
Merrily on steel
I fumbled
As a boat on a rainy stream.
Where innocent feelings
Race to toy.

Any bruise or hurt,
Nor its warnings to heed.
Unbound wings free,
Was all he needed in spree.

The choice made
To miss all fall.
Surely bent
To kiss delightfully the tall.

And as the boy circumvented
To slow,
Moved I away my eyes,
To reminisce in my happy past,
Of 'that child's', bravado!

HIS HORSE GRIEVES

Asking, I neigh. Ahoi!
Do you hear me?
I'm down,
Out of good books of yours,
But not truly out,
Trust me!

Old, weary I.
My place in stable you deny.
How soon you scorn,
'This', your own.

Your love once my own.
Adorns new
Unhearted beast,
As I mourn.
In me you despair,
Not pride least.

My loyal bindings,
Draw me close.
Yet my stride is outsmarted;
Pitfalls, you think,
Are my old gallops.

My heart still frames
Your 'proud win'!
That your grin
Leading my rein,
To cherishing
Prized win.
All smiles you,
My master
For such trophies,
Ever keen.

My blazing bolts,
Their golden sheen,
Past those days, have you seen?

But hello! Your new ride?
It glints, glides, gaily tumbles.
As steel pushes you
Falters downhill.

Watching you ride
In joyful flight,
Swaying in careful delight.

Master, does your heart gallop?
As it now crashes stones,
Fumbles slope?
I, in prayers, am anxious
In dismay;
Will it stop?

Then lo!
Falls beyond,
Downhill, helpless.
Smashing secure.
Clinching breath, I,
In fearful uproar!

But 'it', not caring
If you, my loved master,
Live or die.

I'm in awestruck rue
For what the wretched cycle
Made to you.

Your new love,
Your adore,
How untrue!

DO FURTHER AWAY

The heart then
Wrenched, wrenched,
And wrenched.
The eyes, misty and dense.
Life in shambles
With that blow!
Threat that endangered
Its very existence.

Mind like wild bull,
Midst upmarket stalls,
Played mayhem!

Its tensions to create,
To permeate no peace,
To my uneasy soul;
Bleeding to invisible wounds.
Implacable, Impalpable
Its makers.

No solace, no counsel
To nurture.
Can see blanked out darkness only,
One and another!

Fail, do I?
Pray!
Carry me away,
On further.
To prevail in peace.
My foot falls,
Easy, confident, sure!

THIS BRIDGE; BEYOND

This life, a bridge, yes,
Also said to be conduit.
The links that seem missing,
Are we;
Between life and eternity.

We are eternal,
Is less realized,
But a certainty.

Life, not a puzzle
Or FA query,
But an answer to wisdom
In the cosmos of eternity.
It is an endless entity.

Life, a bubble, a quintessence
Of endlessness.
That does just changes form,
In its shapelessness.

It's the source,
In scintillating grandness,
Of 'the artist' at par in every excellence.

All just energy/light.
Who can determine
Where did it all start and
Where do they arise?

Is, since who knows when,
Been a continuous flow
Of perpetual bliss.
Something that makes
Us ever mesmerized.

Who am I?
And who are you? He?
—Are spiritual,
Awakening questions.

Nameless, endless,
All are 'the same',
In origin, purpose.
Journey chartered out, similarly,
Yet differentiated
By virtue of karma;
We reclaim.

Choices, ourselves in
Lives, previously,
Have, by our thoughts,
Words, deeds;
Summing made.

Below this bridge, its arch,
That flows is the riverine of
Worldly life.
Bearing beautiful us.
Living, loving, having
Our beings,
In constant strife.

We however be,
Rich, pretty,
Powerful or smart.
Yet comes a day,
Calls all to depart!

Sparks of energy ever we.
Lives take on thereafter
To newer enterprises.
Off to newer
And newly made skies.

So, if you'll
Take it from me.
We are
Likened bursts of energies,
Taking on eternal flight.
In every life,
To spread only light!

In sole cosmos,
Are but souls
Of ceaseless love,
We all, absolute delights!

THE LEGEND OF BABU BINOD

He preached with his life—if failed again—
Still not to be fearful, but keep surge on.

To speak up, scold, enrich, nurture with kindness,
Be illumined, strike out ignorance, darkness.

Get, give best of scope for scholastics,
Have life – lessons, carve best, one self.

To love land, the people; not just to scrape ore
But feel much deeper, plenty more.

Hum! The glory of our soil, galore.
Yet keep open hearts' doors.

When pushed, confined; drive away enemies
However mighty, whenever be.

Not to budge but blow the bugle
To summon all zestful minds,

To school, college, university threshold.
Holding arms to dance in a circle.

Of pride, progress, dignity bold—
Such is 'Babu's' legend, lore; raptured, sung, told.

THE BUBBLING BLISS

'The bubbling bliss' of childhood,
Its rosy world of dreamy hues.

Sparkling eyes and naughty smiles,
The jumping jacks and swinging flights.

The open hearts to innocent skies,
of laughter and frolic.

Full of questions, so many queries,
Also sweet excited replies.

My paradise on earth, my childhood days,
When heaven's under the table.

And angelic are my mom's sweet ways,
For any heroic deed, my dad's able.

My imagination, rolls beyond fluffy white clouds,
And in the fairy blue corridor, stays.

LOVE LOST

His handsome features, her pretty graces,
Wed to the night of lights and merriment.

Sub-plot of a fairytale knot,
So far, so good, a love story that would…

But simple the maiden, on night of love;
Innocently unburdened her heavy heart.

All anguish and agonies of her fragile spirit
That had her shattered; Revealed!

Those great efforts only enough, holding her in one piece
Such that the knight had fallen for her.

She emptied her fearful scares; yet courageous dares
To live, love, have home, dreams, and care for herself.

The brave knight though, wasn't brave enough
To match the show.
Dumped her at once, with the least good thought, oh!

Bent in mind 'he', not to love, pained passionate 'she'.
Nor the 'wounded warriors' loving angel be.
So, he went away, to live haplessly, never happier.
Leaving her lonely, whirling strawless in a troubled sea.

TORRENTS; A RAINY AFTERNOON

The earthy scent of my garden
Trailed behind the rains,
To fill the whiff
All around the plot space and beyond.

For, it overflowed a tired soul,
Cascading emotions, vision, reminiscences,
In their fullest flair.
Submerging the soul
In delightful pleasure.

How should I show
My gratefulness, my owe
To torrents just showered;
Pervaded, perfumed, nostalgia more.

LOVE LOST; NOT LORN

Losing love, grateful 'she',
Faced lonely waves of effulgent sea.

Her form sick and scared gently,
Yet she felt it below dignity to beg or plead.

Lending herself to books,
To gain less, but to survive more.

Knew she not, what was to beset her,
However she wrestled, surged, tried being the best.

Taking herself to books, God,
Her goodness, merit, ingenuity put to test.

Learnt well she, fatigued, fought yet,
For a life, as must be.

Again painted she, rosy pictures on canvas heart.
It was all bells, blossoms; considerations fair, smart.

Now she has calling, care, calm caresses;
Her sheer restlessness put to rest.

Loving thoughtfulness put to heart's jest,
Who else can be happier
Than, where women's ventures and god's graces,
Are blended to the best?

CASTLES CRASH

How castles come crashing down,
How winds of change crumble dreams in slumber.

Those slumbers of fleeting moments,
Where the heart laid itself to little rests.

Knowing well of heart's follies
of me and those of mine.

How coveted positions of admirations
stand but on quicksands.

That lofted glory
Those heights of love.

Which were once close to nearness,
Are strangers to all courtesies.

Now not sparing any close signs,
Are only forlorn intimacies.

INNOCENCE FOR BARTER

Chocolates bartered
For innocent smiles,
Innocence in eyes
Lost to those lies.

The warmth of endearment false,
Draws 'wolves' to prey else.
Threatening humanity to tatters,
Building criminal walls
To defend inhumaneness.

Teary humanity can't hide
Scars on its facade.
To find humanity thus blasphemed,
Put to shame;
The elixir of mankind
Where lost? Can any mortal name?

WHEN THE GOING GETS TOUGH

When the going is tough,
I think, refrain for a while,
Lest my efforts go in vain.

My incessant flow of reckless life,
Thinks to apply its brakes on.

Forces me to change on strife,
With calm veneer.

Ponder, to put on my bold reigns,
To get on to where life takes.

To know, to learn flowing on effortless,
Or, to surf all at once on effulgent waves.

Or else, wait for approaching waves to flow by.
Or thoughtless, do I lose out, hidden, shy?

BOOK OF MEMORIES

My memories to self—
The pages of my life-book are almost complete.

Those moments of mistakes when youthful,
And wisdom gathered, there on.

Written pages of my memory-book,
Carved out of mirth, pain, designs, colors, stains.

Those missing pages, when taken ill,
Or suffering any mishap.
Those pages not out of rhyme, reason, will,
Those that only raised tension, bill.

Some pages would've liked erase,
However, it makes my heart hold them close.

As sheer catharsis, to a guilt free self.
For it's my truth, honesty, reality which stays past me.

That's what makes up this Universe,
So, around it goes; I pree.

WHEN ON CLOUD NINE

When now, I'm on cloud nine,
Feel, do I? Do I know? Remember? Do I owe?

Those kind gestures, the worded lips,
Whose help was just at fingertips.

Stairs, that escalator, which lifted-lofted me,
To rise, to reach, to shine better.

The assurance, the counsels
That rubbed off bitter tears.

And helped heal wounds,
To still love life, endear.

Who accepted me,
Whom I simply trust.

Who at night stark, stood nearer,
And though trailing I,
Paced by me,
So as, steps along steps, trod we better.

O! THE BLISSFUL

O! You the blissful most,
A blessing from the heaven's blue,
You sprinkle your divine grace.

And below humanity in mad race,
The world at its puzzled, puzzling maze.

O! Strident people, look not askance;
The comfort to your acid heart,
Is a step closing in; so humanity advance!

The restless streams in you, await
The ocean of selfless love.

Your expanse of trouble, which
In your soul persists,
Is only agony double;
Unless one realizes that Divinity exists.

MOMENTARY MEMORIES

When those, then that were there,
Those, bound by me,
Or those who bound me.

As if, formed droplets upon trees
That trickled,
Dropped as sparkles; faded.

No one moves on their search now,
Unremembered, remains there.

As dust, that hit off hoofs,
Not to besmear, just spread uselessly
Over wagons empty that sway.

Water, like lived memories akin to mine,
Roll down duck-backs, spray.

Not wait or delay
A moment more, or stay.

GO GREEN – MISSION

The domes—green, standing,
Bold, breezy, benignly
Upon those foothills
Beyond the shingly river banks.

Do have, the prowess of easy breath,
To flow through the city lungs.
We should've been grateful for,
If you've ought, 'thanks'
Long before.

Sprawling structures, towers,
Have stolen my green,
As earth loses its splendour,
Its wettest showers.

Nature has hit back,
Thus with oddities.
Floods, famines, aridness
And frequent hurricanes
Simultaneously.

Where once,
The birds twittered,
Butterflies took flight, spread,
Leaves—emerald;
In pouring rains those quivered.

The aroma, aura of
Winding forest path
—To lure the poets,
To sit, walk along blabbering brooks.

Where his hustle-bustle
Thawed, to mumbling
Sporty rivulets.

The cooing, chirping, in
The dense, dark
Forest of yore.
Where humanity
First took birth,
Got nurtured.

Is a gift to the living,
The gratitude of life.

Our greedy self
Having caused much harm,
Now grapples for breath,
As we are grieving, fighting,
Gripping, crippling pandemics.

It's past high-times
When we should've shouldered it,
Woken up by mother nature's clarion.

Now she's stepped out.
Waiting by her depreciating green doors,
The luxurious leafy covers,

The languishing lush meadows,
And sluggish blue waters,
Craving ocean floors.

Ever ready 'she', to lend
Her sustaining hand of help.
We must take her hand,
Weep, repent in her lap.

After this, much harm that's created,
We cannot run off.

Preferably, inevitably,
Ought to restore the oblivion
Of her new-found glory.

So, those who are next,
Reign in prideful moments,
In privileges pristine,
In arms of proud nature!

So, as bask in humanity
create Green-mission;
Her sweet success story,
Chapter of its splendid
Sustainable nature's bounty.

MAKING SOME SENSE

Light is hope.
Life is love.

Promise is eternity.
Peace is breathing calm.

Truth is, that offers no escape.
Honesty, mirror of inner self-scape.

Beauty, that sparks visual pleasure.
Delight lifts spirits, smiling broader.

Earth, a mystery, we owe not own,
In unparalleled cyclic symmetry.

Experiences are our yardsticks
of ageless maturity, ample.

So, business of this world.
It's intricate and nitty-gritty.

Power is fearlessness
Of 'the people', its essence.

Vision is progress.
Steady move of all races.
Nature is life breath for all.
It is not mute witness to human's fall.

God is, all goodness
Perceptible to every sense.

TO THE ONE, MY FRIEND

Coming to me,
I'm your friend;
Full, free and final!

How about you?
Do you think of me,
As such?

These dark evenings,
Grimness reigning supreme,
Does it remind me of you?
I ask myself.

Yes, you,
And only you, I assert.
For all of eternity to listen to.

You, my dear one,
My unknown ally;
'Unknown' though, only to you.

How close
I keep you to my heart,
Only this innerness knows.

You, the spark in my heart,
The frolic in my life,
Many laughters come by.

You, my Lucky charm,
Resort of a soul-wanderer!
Finding my soul linkages in you,
I prosper.

These plunges into ocean time,
With you, my dear twin.
Blending, making this life,
These as if freezed times,
Moments better!

FOR YOU WHO'S RIGHT

If you light up all hearts,
I'm obliged
That you do.

Smiles if broadened,
Horizons if spread,
Life if lifted.

Life surely made sunny
Due to those like
Only you.

It's roots, my belief,
In all that's good.

The 'right' is always
An authority in itself.

The right
That's in our hearts,

The righteous,
To writ upon
All skies,
To shower love, uplift.

And all that's welcome!
That rightfully need be;
Even if, in measures
Tiny, small.
To sum up 'right',
To reign all.

To create canvas sky,
To color darkness dull.

Scaling in heights,
Creating, surpassing
Strong bridges!
Surmounting all of the adverse.

So, life's left to me,
A verse.

In the face of all
That may stand worse.

YOU WON'T KNOW

You know me of course;
My name, my work, my hobbies.
For you, and all,
The same.

But do you know
When I cry
And howl?
You won't.

For I rarely do it, now.
And even if so,
In privacy of
My neat, ironed kerchieves,
Those of which colors?
You mustn't know.

As you won't know
My innermost passions,
And not so its vibrancy.
So, it evoked in my
Choicest colors,
Won't be known to you.

You mostly look into my eye.
But you can't measure
The depths it feels,
The heights it dreams of.

The visions it sustains,
Despite this, my life,
And its bonds those
are fragile!

But tell me,
Do you rarely see me
But only smile?
At everyone, and of course you?

SOFTLY YOU UTTER

As and when
Midst times of fun,
Or at times, when
Annoyance I know all,
And joys I know none,

There comes those whisperings
Into my ears, of
Some, the 'anon'.

Your distant rumble
Or softly spoken words
Of near;

Those that melt into my heart
In gushes of
Unuttered notions.

Words also, which melt the heart in
Unsaid speech, as if – 'morse'
Heaping on, much pleasure,
Respite, ease.

Those glittering passions unknown,
Unguarded flights
of fancies and dreams;
if but once.

Those kindling
Sparkles that flutter
Not fire.
Oh! When you Utter! Same.
The one my name.

If well said to please,
Or may be some far – off Vague utterance,

Or may ev'n it be
Your favourable mumble.
That brings me even closer
To a reality startle.

FRUITION

Talk of ease
If you do, please.
In this unceasing plan
That's nature's boon, bliss.

But now!
These delights,
My, your wanderings, wondrous flights,
Are but a speck,
In the universal scheme, might.
Travels in time's winged sprite.

So, you do obey
But not fear,
Distant rumblings!

Rising waves, at roar.
In the lonesome essence
Of your heart's core.
Ones, that more often
In excitement your heart's stir.

Thoughts, feelings, ideas,
And also churning
Mine, yours, pained plight most.

That skims wasted froth,
Churns up
Smooth heapfuls, clear;
Floating sweet nectar.

Not my illusion,
Are rewards yet unprecedented.
However certain;
In arms of nature's fruition!

BLOWN AS A WISH

This is not something
Which I can get
With ease, at all.
Can't make me happily rich,
Or prosperous
If I sought.

You've to slog against
All rot.

It's not material
Which can be bought,
Or has a tag to it,
Or can be purchased,
And to me, bought,

Neither to be picked at
The supermarket or mall,
Nor online purchases sort.

But has to be carved heartily,
Paid up, in deeds, ideas, thoughts.

Counted as blessings
Has been sacred
Desire in humanity,
From days hoary, old.

Something, I often blow
On my palm,
As coveted wish, untold.

Something, which
However yearned,
Can be called yours.
Only if with practice,
Patience and pains
Have been earned!

This magic is of course,
Being CONTENT;
The overflow of HAPPINESS!
That too blooming
With fragrant VALUES!

That's to be built
Into lives,
Of one and all.

The moral, ethical way
To survive, is the same for all—
Be the rich, snobbish.
Or ones humble,
Wrongly labelled as small.

Sweet are its pleasures;
Their blessings in numbers tall.

Those making you
Definitely better—

A better person, son,
Daughter, teacher,
Father, mother,
Citizen, human!

For your little son,
Small children at school,
You sparkle, as
Their loving icon!

The rewards aren't soon.
But surely are,
An incredible boon!

Makes you cheery, blissful.
Loves and lives upto you.
These virtues,
Your innate, own.

Pulls you up in smiles
In the face of
Biggest troubles.

Will relentlessly
Make you dance
In joy, rock.
Making able you,
To split with laughter,
Makes you sweetly croon!

Giving the lost rot,
Some good shock!

I'M HAPPY TODAY

I'm happy today,
As I am 'one',
Not in painful pieces.

Tears that were,
Have lately dried up, traceless.

The agony of invisible marks, once,
That rose like lava,
To burst open all saved feelings,

Have spread upon
The plain grounds of life.

Long they have laid there,
Thawed now,
After long lasting pain,
Once merciless, raided.

So, I'm happy today,
A solitary volcano, unique
In love piece!
Gaining in
Long lasting freeze.

That's how
Its status now,
As you can only share.
In spirited ecstasy,
And feel just
In heart warming empathy.

The fragmented feeling
That was,
And throttled dreams, once,
Have earned
In silences,
Visions serene.

Spouting colors,
Scented, balmy.

Spreading all over, beyond,
Blending, gushing,
Bold n breezy!

PEARLS OF LOVE

You prevail, you are precious.
Feeling you as I feel no one; I'm serious.

You've touched unknown spots
Of my heart in tenderness.
With you, I'm pure, vibrant love, no less.

A look alone from eyes brown,
Pulls up a smile,
On my glum frown.

Upon your rare loving glance,
Dances this heart on every chance.
And so many heartbeats,
Skip out by chance.

This passing day stream
Invokes in me, winged dreams.

To sail off together, flowing,
In your dreamy dinghy.
Its chance to come out real
Though are tearful few
In my reality.

You speak only words two.
Mine are words full, awaiting queue.
Pouring love to you.

Cascading down this heart,
My love in tumbles
To feel yours
In gushed flows,
Lovingly it rumbles.

I'm still to be here, sure,
For your love to reciprocate.

I'm in my wait
Forever and ever more.
Only for pearls of desire
From love of my life.
Don't you really know who?

FATHERLY CARESSES

To be a father is being divine.
Story of creator, sustainer, protector,
Provider defined.

The strong shelter of our shack,
Where we reside;
Do you know?
It's mercy revisited.

His shades and showers
Of nurture and love unwind,
To glisten it all
Upon our faces, lives.

To send us merrily off to school
That we go, grow, fearless.

His strict rules of conduct,
And counsels against our being undisciplined.

Showers on you blessings now, so lovely
I'm grown up and now to feel
The warmth and heat
That was yours.
And for your great dutiful tasks,
Can find no words.

In this brave,
Brave world, your great endeavours,
I reckon, feel obliged, I'm grateful for.

Your daily tussles
To make all our faces
Happily dazzled.

DUE REVERENCE TO

The teacher whom we pay
Respect, obedience, diligence to—
Most revered in society.
Though not always in the
List of who's who,
Yet builders of all great men—
West or East,
—Aristotle, Chanakya, Panini
Radhakrishnan, at best,
Or others, 'anon',
Millions in number,
Shaping as pillars,
Be of strength.
Behind all achievers,
And great successful women or men,
The architects and designers
Of a nation's might, destiny,
And roaring acclamations.
To such harbinger-teachers,
My palms, I join, in applause,
For their appreciation,
Obeisance, reverence, as I pause.

You Write. We Publish.

To publish your own book, contact us.

We publish poetry collections, short story collections, novellas and novels.

contact@thewriteorder.com

Instagram- thewriteorder

www.facebook.com/thewriteorder

www.ingramcontent.com/pod-product-compliance
Lightning Source LLC
LaVergne TN
LVHW010407070526
838199LV00065B/5909